THE VIRTUAL MUMMY

THE
VIRTUAL
MUMMY

Sarah U. Wisseman

UNIVERSITY OF ILLINOIS PRESS

URBANA AND CHICAGO

Publication of this book was supported by a grant from the
Program on Ancient Technologies and Archaeological Materials
at the University of Illinois at Urbana-Champaign.

♾ This book is printed on acid-free paper.

Library of Congress Cataloging-in-Publication Data
Wisseman, Sarah Underhill.
The virtual mummy / Sarah U. Wisseman.
p. cm.
Includes bibliographical references and index.
ISBN 0-252-02792-2 (cloth : alk. paper)
ISBN 0-252-07100-X (pbk. : alk. paper)
1. Mummies—Egypt. 2. Mummies—Illinois—Urbana. I. Title.
DT62.M7W57   2003
932—dc21   2002004790

For Charlie,
who nicknamed the mummy
"Lazarus"

CONTENTS

PREFACE

DEAD BODIES CANNOT BE TRANSPORTED ACROSS STATE LINES without a death certificate. This little-known law turned out to be crucial in the University of Illinois's acquisition of a mummy in 1989.

Barbara Bohen, then director of the university's World Heritage Museum, had searched long and hard for a human mummy to supplement the animal mummies and burial artifacts in the Egyptian collection. Finally she heard about a Roman-period mummy that had been obtained from the Fayum region of Egypt in the 1920s and kept in a private collection in Illinois for over sixty years. Universities and museums in other states expressed interest in acquiring the mummy, but how could they move it without a death certificate? It could not be unwrapped, and it was doubtful that any physician would write a death certificate for a body he could not examine. Clearly, it was easier to keep the mummy within Illinois than move it out of state, and the major research university in Urbana-Champaign would be the ideal final home for the mummy. Thus the mummy came to the museum, now known as the Spurlock Museum.

My first news of the mummy's arrival was a phone call in 1989 from James Dengate, a classics professor and a curator at the museum: "Sarah, we have a mummy!" We convened key members of our Program on Ancient Technologies and Archaeological Materials (ATAM) to meet with museum staff. We discussed what might be learned about the mummy without mistreating the human remains or damaging the display quality of the artifact. Who was the person inside the wrappings? What was his or her social status, age, diet, medical history, and cause of death? What could we learn about the embalming fluids and mummification techniques used in the Roman period compared to those of earlier times? We already knew something about what could be done with medical imaging techniques, but were there other essentially nondestructive possibilities? Director Bohen gave us permission to conduct a variety of tests on the mummy. She also gave us a time limit: the mummy, along with at least some of the research results, would be displayed in a new exhibit, *Bound for Eternity,* the following year.

The Virtual Mummy is the story of the interdisciplinary research project that grew out of that initial meeting. ATAM recruited physicians and technicians in two local hospitals and researchers in classics, anthropology, chemistry, veterinary medicine, entomology, textile sciences, supercomputing, and other units at the University of Illinois at Urbana-Champaign to work on the mummy project. The full list of participants is in the Acknowledgments. Two videotapes, several technical articles, a book chapter, and an article in the popular magazine *Discover* (July 1991) resulted from this research and told parts of our story. Some of the more technical materials are fairly inaccessible for the general public.

This book gives a complete account for the first time, and it is intended for a diverse audience of museum visitors, teachers, and students who are interested in Egyptian mummies. In order not to break the flow of the story, references are not included in the text, but sources appear in the bibliography at the end of the book. Useful Web sites on mummification and ancient Egypt are included.

ACKNOWLEDGMENTS

THIS BOOK, LIKE MOST BOOKS, COULD NOT HAVE BEEN WRITTEN without assistance from key institutions and individuals. I owe special thanks to the Spurlock Museum and its staff, especially the former director, Barbara Bohen, and one of its curators, James Dengate, for access to the mummy. I also thank Linda Klepinger and Mary Hynes (Anthropology and ATAM) for timely editing and helpful suggestions; Douglas Brewer (current director, Spurlock Museum) for reviewing chapters 1 and 3; Carter Lupton and Bob Brier, who read and commented on the entire manuscript (I am especially grateful to Carter for additional bibliography); and all of the participants in the mummy research listed below for their generous donations of time and expertise. All units are at the University of Illinois at Urbana-Champaign (UIUC) unless otherwise noted.

X-RAY RADIOGRAPHY AND CT SCANNING
Richard Keen, Veterinary Medicine, UIUC
Joseph Barkmeier, M.D., Carle Clinic, Urbana, Illinois

3-D IMAGING AND RECONSTRUCTION
Clint Potter, Rachael Brady, and David Lawrance, National Center for Supercomputing Applications (NCSA), UIUC
Raymond Evenhouse, School of Biomedical and Health Information Sciences, University of Illinois at Chicago, and MicroCut Engineering, Streamwood, Illinois

TEXTILE ANALYSIS
Mastura Raheel, Textile Sciences, Natural Resources and Environmental Sciences, UIUC

BONE AND TEETH ANALYSIS
Linda Klepinger, Anthropology, UIUC
Stanley Ambrose, Anthropology, UIUC
William Hutchinson, D.D.S., Champaign, Illinois
Morgan Powell, D.D.S., Champaign, Illinois

RESIN ANALYSIS
Mark Proefke and Kenneth Rinehart, Chemistry, UIUC

WOOD ANALYSIS AND RADIOCARBON DATING
Jack Liu and Dennis Coleman, Illinois State Geological Survey
Roger DeChamps, Musée Royal de L'Afrique Centrale, Belgium

INSECT ANALYSIS
John Bouseman, Illinois State Natural History Survey

STUCCO ANALYSIS
Alwyn Eades, Alan Kahn, and Richard Haasch, Materials Research Laboratory,
    UIUC

DNA ANALYSIS
Ingolf Thuesen and Henrik Nielsen, Carsten Niebuhr Institute of Ancient
    Near Eastern Studies, Copenhagen

PROJECT COORDINATION
Sarah Wisseman, Program on Ancient Technologies and Archaeological
    Materials (ATAM), UIUC
James Dengate, Classics and ATAM, UIUC
Barbara Bohen, Spurlock (World Heritage) Museum, UIUC

Special thanks to the Large Animal Clinic, College of Veterinary Medicine,
UIUC; Covenant Hospital, Champaign; and Carle Clinic, Urbana, for technical support and the use of X-ray, CT scanning, and MRI equipment; and
to the Office of the Chancellor and the College of Liberal Arts and Sciences
at the University of Illinois; Friends of the Spurlock (World Heritage) Museum; Champaign Rotary Club; and Harlan and Pam Berk, University of
Illinois alumni, for invaluable assistance in the acquisition and transportation of the mummy.

THE VIRTUAL MUMMY

INTRODUCTION

RECENT INVESTIGATIONS OF THE AUSTRIAN ICEMAN, THE PERUVIAN Ice Maiden, and the Danish bog bodies have raised public awareness about what can be learned from studying ancient human remains. Bodies —especially mummified ones—contain a wealth of information on ancient health, disease, genetics, and diet that can be recovered with modern technology. The archaeological contexts of bodies are equally important. The tombs, grave markers, burial wrappings or coffins, and any accompanying pottery, jewelry, weapons, and other items are essential for reconstructing aspects of daily life as well as burial ritual, religious beliefs, social organization, and economics.

Rich graves have been systematically robbed throughout history in many parts of the world. Beginning in antiquity, tomb robbers removed gold artifacts and fine ceramics from Egyptian and Etruscan tombs for quick sale. Modern treasure hunters and dealers in illegal antiquities have continued the practice of separating valuable grave goods from their bodies, with the result that archaeological context has been completely lost for many of these objects.

In Egypt, sometimes the practice was reversed: the bodies—mummies— were removed leaving tombs, markers, and grave goods behind. In the Middle Ages, mummies were exported by the ton to Europe to be ground up for medicinal powders to treat stomach ailments and ointments to stop bruising. "Mummy" was so popular a cure that a fake version, sometimes no more than a mixture of pitch and herbs, was a hot commodity.

Thousands of Egyptian mummies have been destroyed in one way or another. Mummies were pulverized to make paper in Maine. According to

Mark Twain's tongue-in-cheek comment in *Innocents Abroad,* mummies were also used as locomotive fuel. Roman-period face portraits were ripped off their mummies to sell to art dealers, and then the mummies were discarded. Choice mummies were exported to Europe to supply entertainment at social gatherings. One notorious invitation, dated 1850, reads "A mummy from Thebes to be unrolled at half-past Two" (figure 1). The mummy was discarded after ceremonial unwrapping, thus making any further study impossible.

It was not until the late nineteenth and early twentieth centuries that Egyptian mummies became the subjects of careful investigation rather than mere objects of curiosity. Interested scholars unwrapped mummies in order to study the preservation of the bodies inside and any evidence of the embalming methods. Investigators quickly discovered how difficult it was to rewrap a mummy after such an unveiling; some mummies were so solidified from the hardening of resins and other embalming fluids that they required a chisel or a saw for opening. Needless to say, the remains were hardly displayable in a museum.

With all this activity, it is surprising that there are so many Egyptian

FIGURE 1 Invitation from Lord Londesborough (From C. El Mahdy, *Mummies, Myth and Magic,* p. 176. Reprinted with permission of Geoffrey T. Martin)

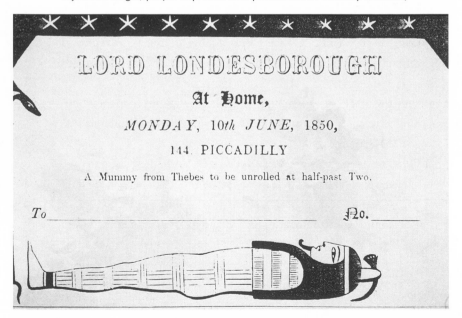

mummies left in museums today. Even a scientific unwrapping removes one more mummy—or at least the context of its wrappings—from those available for future display. Taking destructive samples of any kind is usually forbidden because it alters the artifact in an irreversible way. Also, because of the increased awareness of laws such as the Native American Graves Protection and Repatriation Act (NAGPRA) in the United States, curators are reluctant to do anything that might be interpreted as disrespectful treatment of human remains.

The University of Illinois mummy project was one of the first nondestructive investigations of an Egyptian mummy conducted in the United States, combining respectful treatment of human remains with the preservation of the mummy for museum exhibits (figure 2). No autopsy or unwrapping was performed, and the only materials that were sampled were scraps obtained from the lower end of the mummy where the wrappings were already loose and foot bones protruded.

The other noteworthy feature of our interdisciplinary study was that it employed a combination of three-dimensional reconstruction techniques

FIGURE 2 Richard Keen positioning the Spurlock mummy for X ray (Courtesy College of Veterinary Medicine, University of Illinois at Urbana-Champaign [UIUC])

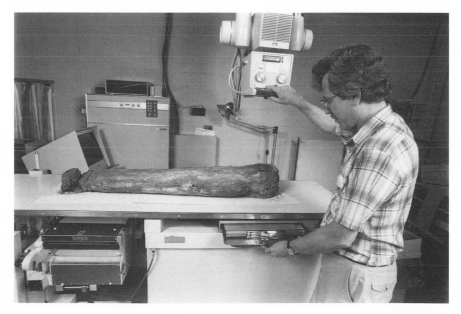

using CT scan data. Although such computer manipulations have now become standard, our team was the first to use a supercomputer for volumetric rendering of the mummy's head and torso. Using software created in the University of Illinois National Center for Supercomputing Applications (NCSA), David Lawrance, a physician, did a "virtual" autopsy by computer, gradually stripping off layers to reveal what was underneath. In a separate effort, the head was sculpted—literally putting the flesh back on the bones—using the CT data plus ultrasound data from living populations to obtain approximate tissue depths. The resulting head is much more lifelike than earlier mummy reconstructions using measurements derived from corpses. The skull was constructed by a medical artist, Raymond Evenhouse, first by hand and later by stereolithography—a technique in which a computer-controlled laser beam generates the skull out of a vat of liquid plastic.

A primary project goal was to investigate the age, sex, health, diet, disease, and cause of death of the individual inside the wrappings without destroying the mummy. Our team of archaeologists and scientists was also interested in studying the embalming methods to see how they differed from those of other mummies of the same and earlier periods. Finally, we hoped to discover if the internal evidence matched that of the exterior wrappings and our preliminary conclusion that the mummified person came from the upper stratum of Egyptian society of about A.D. 100.

1

PREPARATION FOR

THE AFTERLIFE

THE EGYPTIANS BELIEVED IN AN AFTERLIFE THAT WAS VERY SIMILAR
to life before death. The Egyptian soul had three parts, the *ka,* the *ba,* and
the *akh.* The ka was essentially a person's double, one that had physical
needs after death. The ba, often depicted as a human-headed bird hovering over the mummy, was the part of the soul that moved between the
worlds of the living and the dead (figure 3). The akh was the transfigured
spirit that survived death and mingled with the gods.

Preparation for the afterlife included preserving the deceased's physical remains as a home for the ka and providing bread, beer, oxen, and fowl
to feed it. In addition, the preserved body—the mummy—had to be recognizable so that the ka could identify it and the ba could return to it each
night after spending time in the sunshine.

Everything that had been necessary in life—food, drink, servants, weapons, jewelry, and clothes—was placed in the tomb to sustain the deceased
in the afterlife. Paintings or other representations could substitute for the
real thing on occasion; for example, *shabti* (workers who would labor in
place of the deceased in the afterlife) were often supplied in the form of
small statues.

Preservation of the body was achieved in several ways. The earliest
mummies from the Predynastic period (before 3050 B.C.) were not em-

FIGURE 3 Ba-bird hovering over a mummy (After the papyrus of Ani from Thebes, ca. 1420 B.C.)

balmed. Instead, they were formed by natural desiccation of bodies that were buried in shallow graves in the hot, dry desert sand. In later periods, bodies laid out in tombs decayed because moisture-laden air could reach the tissues. The Egyptians gradually developed an elaborate procedure for halting decay, drying and preserving the entire body, and restoring the appearance of life to the wrapped form by using a variety of stuffing and packing materials.

Our two primary sources of information about mummification are from literary descriptions of mummification and from the mummies themselves. The best-known descriptions are by Herodotus, a fifth-century B.C. Greek historian, and Diodorus Siculus, a first-century B.C. Greek writer. There are also some first-century A.D. papyri that record spells for the embalmers to recite while bandaging.

The organs most likely to decay (intestines, liver, lungs, and stomach) were removed from the body as early as the Fourth Dynasty through a slit in the abdomen, usually on the left side. The brain, an organ of unknown function to the Egyptians, was removed perhaps as early as the Twelfth Dynasty and certainly by the beginning of the Eighteenth Dynasty (New

Kingdom) by punching a hole through the bone at the back of the nose. Embalmers usually left the heart in place because they thought it was the seat of the soul and the intellect.

Although mummification techniques reached their peak during the Twenty-first Dynasty (tenth century B.C.), it is the New Kingdom (Eighteenth to Twentieth Dynasties, or 1549–1069 B.C.) procedures for mummification that are the best known and most frequently described. After evisceration, the body cavity was cleansed with water and palm wine and packed with aromatics and temporary stuffing (for example, bags of sawdust or myrrh). Then the body was completely covered with mounds of a natural salt called natron. After about a month, the natron was removed, the temporary stuffing extracted, and the body cavity cleansed a second time. Next, the brain cavity was filled with resin-impregnated cloth; the body repacked with sawdust, linen, lichens, sand, or mud; and the skin anointed with resins, honey, and other fragrant substances. The nose was plugged and the eyelids were plumped up with cloth pads or onions. Finally, the body was wrapped in yards and yards of linen, with fingers, toes, arms, and legs separately bandaged. Amulets—protective charms made out of faience (a quartz-based ceramic) or stone—were inserted between the layers.

New Kingdom mummies show evidence of special cosmetic attention. Women with sparse hair had extra locks woven in with their natural hair. Nails were often painted, especially on royal mummies, and at least one mummy had its hair dyed (hennaed).

According to Herodotus, the entire mummification process took approximately seventy days (this has recently been verified by Bob Brier's experiments with making a modern mummy). This elaborate procedure, initially applied only to royalty, was later extended to the middle and lower classes.

The account of Herodotus also indicates that the degree of care taken by the embalmers was directly related to a client's purse. Those who could afford to pay received elaborate mummies, complete with amulets, nail covers, deluxe packing materials, and full wrapping with many yards of fabric. Clients who had only modest funds received a reduced embalming job, with less attention paid to preserving the viscera, cheaper packing materials, and no wrapping. Instead of having the organs that caused decay removed, such mummies might receive only a corrosive enema using cedar (or juniper) oil followed by drying in natron. The poorest clients could expect only an intestinal purge (with a salt solution rather than the expensive cedar oil) and drying before the body was returned to its relatives. While the mummies of wealthy or royal clients were wrapped in specially commissioned cloth beginning in the late Eighteenth Dynasty, mummies of commoners were often wrapped in household linen. A mummy in the Guimet Museum of Natural History in Lyons, France, was wrapped in a sail—suggesting that the person inside was a sailor or a boat owner.

Some additional details about mummification emerge from other ancient writers. Diodorus Siculus writes that a scribe traced the incision where the cut was to be made for evisceration (the man who actually made the cut was supposed to flee the premises). He also records that embalmers, who operated in guilds, were honored and respected men. The same writer says bitumen was imported from the Dead Sea for use by Egyptian embalmers, but bitumen was used far less commonly than were various resins from pine, fir, or cedar trees. Two other writers mention the viscera: Plutarch (first to second century A.D.) says they were thrown into the Nile, but Porphyry (third century A.D.) says they were removed and put in a canopic chest.

Archaeological excavations and examinations of mummies have revealed that over their three-thousand-year history, mummification practices underwent many modifications. The accumulating evidence shows that during any given time period, several different techniques were used. This may be due to economics or geographical variation as much as to customary practice, just as Herodotus suggested with his three methods that varied in cost.

During both the Middle Kingdom (2066–1650 B.C.) and the Late Period (525–332 B.C.), the internal organs were sometimes removed *per anum*—through the anal passage. The viscera were not always treated separately and placed in canopic jars; during some dynasties, they were wrapped in small packages and returned to the body cavity or placed between the mummy's legs. The brain, when it was removed, was sometimes replaced by liquid resin rather than resin-soaked linen. Amulets were not common after the Ptolemaic period.

The mummies also show considerable variation in how the linen shrouds were decorated. External ornament began with plaster modeling of facial features over the bandages in the Archaic and Old Kingdom periods, changing to masks, anthropoid coffins, full-length mummy boards, and beaded nets in later periods. Painted decoration varied from the elaborate feathers on Seventeenth Dynasty coffins to vignettes of the major gods and goddesses associated with death and the afterlife. These include Osiris (the major god, usually shown as a mummy); Isis (both sister and wife to Osiris); Nephthys (a goddess who helps watch over Osiris); Anubis (the jackal-headed god of embalming); and Horus (a falcon-headed sky god and son of Osiris) and his four sons. Nut (the sky goddess) also appears on mummies and coffins from the Eighteenth Dynasty on. Nut is usually shown winged, standing or kneeling above representations of the crossed bands that hold the shroud in place.

By the Roman period (30 B.C.–A.D. 395), both the external and the internal mummy had changed because embalmers had different priorities. They took shortcuts, such as not removing the viscera at all and pouring quantities of molten resin over the body rather than taking the time to thoroughly dry and preserve it. Instead, they concentrated on making the exterior of the mummy look good, using decorative wrapping patterns, gold leaf, and tinted stucco in addition to mummy portraits. The result was some of the most spectacular mummies on display in museums today.

2

A SHORT HISTORY OF

MUMMY STUDIES

IT WAS NOT UNTIL KONRAD VON RÖNTGEN'S DISCOVERY OF X RAYS in 1895 that doctors and other scientists were able to examine mummies nondestructively. X-ray radiography, now a standard medical technique, is used to investigate growth stages, fractures, and signs of disease. X rays penetrate the object from the top down or from side to side and are registered on a photographic film placed behind the object. Different materials absorb different amounts of X rays and these variations appear as contrasting dark and light areas on the X-ray film. Reading the X rays is like viewing a negative instead of a positive picture: the densest materials such as bone and metal are white, the thinner materials are gray, and empty space is black. Even though X rays can be difficult to interpret since the viewer is seeing all the layers at once, many doctors and physical anthropologists still prefer plain radiographs to CT scans for evaluating age and evidence of disease.

Sir Flinders Petrie, the famous Egyptologist who pioneered the use of ceramic seriation and stratigraphy in archaeology, was among the first to X-ray a mummy, in 1898. Shortly after this, in 1903, X rays were used to radiograph the mummy of Pharaoh Thutmosis IV. Since no other transport was available, the investigators (the anatomist Grafton Elliot Smith and the archaeologist Howard Carter) took the dead pharaoh in a horse-drawn cab to a nearby nursing home for the X rays and then returned the patient to the Cairo Museum the same way.

By the 1930s, X-ray radiography was a common method used to non-destructively survey mummies. R. L. Moodie used it on both Egyptian and Peruvian mummies in the Field Museum of Natural History in Chicago.

The complete collection of royal mummies in the Cairo Museum was X-rayed in the 1960s by a team of dentists and other scientists from the University of Michigan's School of Dentistry, backed by Alexandria University and the U.S. Health Service. This team, led by James E. Harris, Kent Weeks, and Edward Wente, was particularly interested in how radiography could contribute to the study of dental health and disease. They found evidence of cavities, abscesses, and worn-down teeth, plus plenty of signs of disease.

The ninety-year-old Ramesses II had severe tooth wear, caused by eating bread made out of stone-ground wheat. The grit incorporated into the flour during grinding, plus any stray sand that was blowing around, wore teeth down like sandpaper. This kind of tooth wear has shown up in many other Egyptian mummies since bread was a staple of the Egyptian diet.

Ramesses II also had hardening of the arteries (arteriosclerosis). Another pharaoh, Siptah, had a foot deformity probably caused by polio or cerebral palsy. Age assessments of other pharaohs (based on measuring fusion in the growth plates at the end of the long bones as well as tooth wear) led to reevaluation of the identity and age of some of the bodies and controversy about the length of their reigns.

Other scientists heard of these discoveries and were eager to set up their own mummy projects. Some found (to their surprise) that they were not the first to investigate their chosen mummies. When the paleopathologist Aidan Cockburn and his colleagues autopsied a mummy in the Detroit Institute of Arts in the early 1970s, they found an ancient-looking piece of paper inside. It turned out to be an English tide table dating to the 1800s rather than an Egyptian papyrus. In Liverpool, an X ray taken in 1966 revealed a surgical scoop lost by a surgeon who had helped examine the same mummy in 1851.

The Manchester University Museum actually conducted two projects, separated in time by several decades. A team led by Margaret Murray in 1908 carefully unwrapped two Twelfth Dynasty mummies, the "Two Brothers" mummies. Lung tissue samples from these mummies were kept until the 1970s, when microscopy revealed severe pneumoconiosis (silicosis).

The second Manchester Museum project, during the 1970s, led by Dr. Rosalie David, generated considerable data on mummies' ages, injuries, diseases, and causes of death. Radiocarbon dating of Manchester Museum mummy 1770 suggested that the fifteen-year-old girl inside was rewrapped in the Ptolemaic period. Her internal organs and lower limbs were missing, and the embalmers seemed to have been unsure that she was female: they provided both nipple covers and a false phallus. Most of the Manchester data was published in *The Manchester Museum Mummy Project* (1979) or in later volumes edited by R. David such as the symposium proceedings *Science in Egyptology* (1986).

In Philadelphia, investigation of a Ptolemaic mummy, PUM II (Pennsylvania University Museum II), found organ packages in the abdomen and thorax containing spleen, intestine, and lung tissues. Scanning electron microscopy (SEM) revealed the blowfly and a Dermestes beetle, flesh-eating insects who took up residence in the mummy at different times as the body decomposed. Intestinal parasites such as guinea worm and liver fluke were found as well. PUM II also had carbon particles in his lungs—the evidence of the disease anthrocosis, one suffered by modern coal miners.

Further advances in mummy investigation coincided with the introduction of a new imaging instrument, the CAT or CT scanner. CAT stands for Computerized Axial Tomography and is a kind of X ray in the round. The CT scanner, in use since the 1960s, yields cross-sectional slices through a body rather than anterior-posterior or lateral views, enabling researchers to better visualize fractures, specific organs, and layering of tissues and wrappings without damaging the mummies. CT slices can also be stacked and combined to produce three-dimensional models.

Mummy projects over the past thirty years have made full use of nondestructive imaging techniques, radiography and CT scanning, as well as full autopsies or selective tissue sampling. Projects in Philadelphia, Boston, Lyons, and elsewhere have employed various types of microscopy, spectroscopy, and endoscopy to study both ancient tissues and the composition of embalming materials, especially resins.

These various projects have all contributed to a greater or lesser degree to the body of knowledge about ancient Egyptian diseases, trauma, and causes of death during different periods. Arthritis, a disease of the joints suffered today, was very common. Examinations of mummies in Toronto and the British Museum in London showed evidence of trichinosis and malaria. Some mummies, such as the Seventeenth Dynasty ruler Seqenenre Tao, exhibited severe head trauma from battle or the blows of an assassin. Schistosomiasis, a parasitic disease also known as bilharzia, was another common ailment.

Both destructive and nondestructive scientific studies have turned up interesting facts about the variability of mummification practices in every period. The heart was not always left inside the body by the embalmers when other organs were removed. X rays and CT scans occasionally reveal empty chest cavities, probably due to accidental rather than intentional heart removal.

Imaging studies of mummies in Milwaukee and elsewhere have shown extensive variation in mummification techniques, especially in Ptolemaic and Roman mummies. The brain was sometimes removed through the base of the skull rather than through the nose. CT slices show instances of solidified resin (rather than resin-soaked cloth) filling the cranium, for example, in the Ptolemaic mummy of Wenuhotep at the Indianapolis Children's Museum. Mummies in Toronto, Cleveland, Dayton, and Boston show evidence of no brain removal at all. Similarly, abdominal incisions have been found in the center of the body or on the right side instead of on the left.

Another discovery is that wrappings do not always reflect what is beneath the surface. Some mummies have been rewrapped in antiquity and more than one body has been found inside a single wrapping. Fake or partially fake mummies also occur. A supposed human infant mummy turned out to be mummified cats, and a child mummy in Bristol turned out to be a jumble of bones—from several children. Finally, in Roman mummies, the age and sex of the individual depicted in the face portrait frequently does not match that of the body inside the wrappings.

Mummies varied enormously in their degree of preservation. Flesh-eating beetles found inside many Ptolemaic and Roman mummies indicate considerable decomposition prior to wrapping. Desiccation was not always completed before wrapping; mummies in Wisconsin museums show signs of drying and shrinking of the tissues after wrapping. Inept desiccation and decay prevention can be explained by the shortcuts taken by Roman-period embalmers: not removing the viscera and pouring quantities of resin over the body rather than stuffing it with preservative substances.

Mummies from Duch, a site in the Kharga oasis of the Libyan desert, were found already stripped of their wrappings and adornments. Despite systematic pillaging, the stiffened bodies were well-enough preserved that modern workers could carry them around as easily as department store manikins and lay them out in rows for examination. These remains of hardworking commoners have been studied extensively by Françoise Dunand and Roger Lichtenberg. The mummies showed evidence of their arduous lifestyles and short life spans: extensive arthritis, scoliosis, fractures, and parasitic diseases. One child mummy had a fractured skull (just like our mummy) and died because of it. Other findings include lines (striations) on the long bones from periods of arrested growth, interpreted as evidence of malnutrition and food shortage.

The Duch mummies—all dating roughly to the period of Roman occupation of Egypt (first century B.C.–fifth century A.D.)—show that mummification practices varied according to economic considerations, just as Herodotus described in his fifth-century B.C. *Histories.* Of the bodies that were mummified, removal of the brain was common but abdominal evisceration was quite rare. Treatments ranged from very rudimentary mummification to elaborate gilding of the body and the face.

Scientific investigations of mummies continue today with a new emphasis on nondestructive analyses and preserving the mummies for future researchers and museum visitors. Gradually we are uncovering more and more about the health and disease of pharaohs, but we are also learning about the hardships of daily life experienced by pyramid builders, bakers and beer brewers, and laborers of every class.

3

PROVENANCE AND

ICONOGRAPHY

WHO WAS THE PERSON INSIDE THE SPURLOCK MUSEUM MUMMY, and where did he live and die? What was his cultural background and social status?

Unfortunately our mummy has no secure provenance—site of origin and burial context—or any inscription or other label identifying the individual inside. All we know is that the mummy came from an unknown burial in the Fayum.

PHYSICAL AND HISTORICAL SETTING

The Fayum is a fertile depression located southwest of the Nile delta with a long history of Graeco-Roman settlement (figure 4). It is one of the three major cultivable areas of Egypt along with the Nile valley and the Nile delta. This area, originally settled and ruled by Egyptians, was taken over by Greeks along with the rest of Egypt at the beginning of the Ptolemaic period in 332 B.C. At the same time, a new capital was created at Alexandria.

Although Egyptians continued to live in the Fayum, the large influx of Greek settlers changed the political and social landscape. Many of these settlers were Greek mercenaries who had fought for Alexander the Great. They were rewarded for their service with Fayum land grants, which then

MEDITERRANEAN SEA

Alexandria

Naukratis

Cairo

Saqqara ● ● Memphis

Fayum

el-Hibeh

Oxyrhynchus ●

Antinoopolis

Tuna el-Gebel ●

FIGURE 4 Map of lower Egypt and the Fayum

became family property that was passed down to their descendants. The enhanced prosperity and political stability of the Fayum under the Ptolemies drew other immigrants—Jews, Syrians, and Libyans—who further increased the local population and intermarried with Egyptians.

Under Greek rule, inhabitants of the larger towns adopted many Greek customs, including Greek education for youths and Greek personal names. Cultural transmission went the other way as well. Greeks and their families revered Egyptian gods, to whom they gave new (Greek) names. Greeks also adopted Egyptian funerary practices and mummified many of their dead. Some of these Greek mummies have been identified by the Greek names inscribed on the wrappings or on separate wooden labels attached to the bodies.

By the time of Cleopatra's death and the beginning of Roman rule in 30 B.C., the population of the Fayum was diverse. This cultural melting pot allowed an unusual coexistence of Greek education and language, Roman government, and widespread adoption of Egyptian religious beliefs and funerary customs.

Egyptians with Greek family ties viewed themselves as Greeks, but Roman administrators thought otherwise. Egyptians were Egyptians, even if they were married to Greeks. Whether or not one was a Roman citizen was the important issue. Greeks were grouped with Egyptians (noncitizens), unless they lived in the largely Greek cities of Alexandria, Ptolemais, Naukratis, and Antinoopolis. These Greeks did not have to pay the poll tax imposed on all other male inhabitants. Although Romans enjoyed the highest privileges, Greeks were eligible for Roman administrative posts. Greeks, Egyptians, and others could achieve Roman military status, and Egyptians who served in the Roman army could eventually become Roman citizens.

Funerary customs incorporated some new elements during the first and second centuries A.D. Romans (and probably Greeks who wanted to emulate their Roman rulers) adopted the practice of mummification, but they often replaced earlier cartonnage (papyrus or cloth mixed with plaster or adhesives) head and foot pieces with Roman-style portraits painted in encaustic (hot wax mixed with colored pigments) inserted into the mummy wrappings (figure 5). The lower portions of these mummies varied, but many of them were decorated with typical Egyptian scenes associated with death and preparation for the afterlife.

Roman portraits were expensive status symbols. Clearly not everyone could afford such a portrait or the elaborate funeral that normally accompanied a high-quality mummy. Letters on papyri dating to the late Ptolemaic and Roman periods describe the high cost of funerals, including itemized lists of embalming materials (wax, resins, linen, red pigment), female mourners, and transportation by donkey. The total expense has been estimated at almost two years' salary for most people, a sum that only upper and upper middle classes could afford.

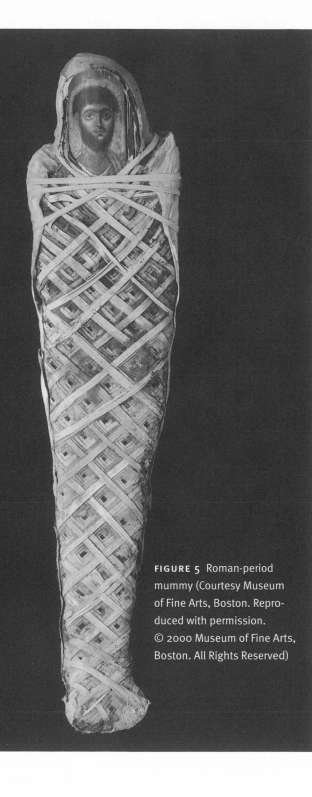

The cemeteries of the Fayum have produced many "Fayum portraits" but few complete mummies. Our mummy, although complete, is far from being the best-preserved example of mummies from the Roman period (figure 6). Much of its face portrait is lost, and the wrappings around the feet are so loose that bits of bone, cloth, and hardened resin have fallen out (plate 1). Did the damage to the mummy occur in ancient times, before it was buried, or in modern times, before the mummy arrived at the Spurlock Museum? To what extent can we retrace its travels?

The most famous Fayum cemeteries are Hawara, near the town of Arsinoë, and el-Rubayat, near Philadelphia. Since early collectors sought high-quality art that was easily transported to Europe, they often took portrait panels and ignored the mummies. The Viennese antiquities dealer Theodor Graf was a typical collector. He purchased portraits that had been removed from their mummies by Bedouin salt miners working at el-Rubayat during the late 1880s. The mummies were left behind and their archaeological contexts were never recorded.

The exception to the rule was Sir Flinders Petrie, who scientifically excavated complete mummies at Hawara in the late nineteenth century and meticulously recorded their provenance. A few other complete mummies had been collected from Sakkara in 1615 and later at el-Hibeh (a site located on the east bank of the Nile, slightly south of the Fayum). These mummies were found in batches in shallow, unmarked graves, caves, brick chambers, and reused tombs. Occasionally they were found buried singly in wooden coffins or inserted under the floors of buildings.

Mummies with portraits may have been kept in private sepulchers or special rooms in people's houses for the family to visit, with final burial delayed by many years. This practice, described in contemporary literary sources on papyri, presumably had its origin in Roman ancestor worship. Greek and Roman writers describe mummies standing upright in wooden coffins or against walls. There is some supportive evidence from archaeology: tall, narrow wooden cupboards with doors have been found, and Petrie found mummies at Hawara that showed considerable damage around the feet and ankles. Wear and tear included cuts and abrasions in the wrappings, water damage, and even graffiti. Petrie concluded that

FIGURE 6 Spurlock
Museum mummy
(Courtesy B. Wiegand,
UIUC News Bureau)

these mummies were placed upright in homes in high-traffic areas so the living could visit them easily. According to Petrie, the discrepancy between the careful preparation of the mummies and their hasty, unorganized burials could be explained if families kept the mummies in their homes as long as the living had any interest in them—perhaps for as long as a generation or two. When the mummies were soiled and broken and their people forgotten, they were discarded.

The damage to the Spurlock mummy's lower end certainly recalls the findings of Petrie, but we do not know when or how this damage occurred. The mummy may have been stored upright in Roman times or more recently before it was acquired by the Spurlock Museum.

ICONOGRAPHY AND STYLISTIC DATE

Mummy portraits often look very realistic, but not all of them were painted from life. Wooden picture frames found at Hawara (figure 7) support the idea that some of these portraits were commissioned during people's lifetimes, removed from the wall and trimmed at the time of death, and inserted in the mummy wrappings. Yet it is unlikely that everyone had time

FIGURE 7 Wooden picture frame found at Hawara (After W. F. Petrie, *Hawara, Biahmu, and Arsinoë* [London, 1889], pl. 12)

21

or money for such advance planning—especially when a child died—so some portraits were probably purchased from stock or commissioned after death. Portraits vary from the ideally beautiful (regular features with no blemishes) to fairly stark portrayals of gray hair and moles.

The iconography of the portraits mixes Egyptian, Greek, and Roman elements, thus providing clues for dating the associated mummies. Jewelry, dress, and hairstyles reflect current fashion and can often be linked with customary attire during the reigns of specific Roman emperors.

The Spurlock mummy, like many other mummies dating to the Roman period, has a Roman-style face portrait inserted into wrappings that have been coated with a red-tinted stucco (plate 2). The poorly preserved portrait shows a youth with dark, curly hair, crowned with a gold laurel wreath and wearing a white garment, a himation, with a dark stripe. The garb appears to be typically male dress, but we cannot be certain this is a young man since women are sometimes shown wearing the same costume. The details of the eyes, nostrils, and lips are visible under ultraviolet light but difficult to see otherwise.

Below the face portrait on the Spurlock mummy are registers of Egyptian gods commonly associated with burial and rebirth (figure 8). At the top are *wadjet* (eyes, associated with Horus, the god of the sky and the son of Osiris and Isis) (plate 3). The eyes have a protective function, symbolizing the health and revitalization of the dead person in the afterlife; they can also be interpreted as the signs for the natural cycles of the sun and the moon. Just below are two falcons, representations of Horus in his falcon form. Below the falcons stands Nut, the sky goddess, who was the mother of Isis, Osiris, Nephthys, and Seth. Nut holds the feathers of Maat, the goddess (and also the concept) of truth, order, and balance. Above Nut's head is a sun disk, just as on a cartonnage in the University Museum in Philadelphia and on a Roman-period mummy in Cambridge, England. Near the feet of the mummy is Osiris, the major god associated with both death and the afterlife (plate 4). Since he was the first mummy (reassembled and wrapped by Isis, his sister-wife, after their jealous brother Seth killed Osiris and cut him up), Osiris is often depicted as a mummy on mummy shrouds and in other types of funerary art.

Many features of the Spurlock mummy, especially the style of the portrait and the specific Egyptian gods depicted in the lower registers, have

FIGURE 8 Spurlock Museum mummy, sketch made under ultraviolet light (Courtesy A. Tsakiropolou)

parallels in mummies from Hawara, now in museums in Evanston (Illinois), Copenhagen, Manchester, and London. Manchester Museum mummy 1775, dated to the early second century A.D., has a very similar decorative scheme of Horus falcons, Osiris, and a standing Nut with sun disk and feathers (figure 9).

Mummy portraits from el-Hibeh have gold lozenges like those painted around the face portrait on the shroud of the Spurlock mummy, and similar folds at the top of the mummy. The best example (almost certainly from el-Hibeh) is in the J. Paul Getty Museum in Malibu, California (figure 10).

The Hawara and el-Hibeh mummies all date to the late first or early second century (about A.D. 100) and provide a good basis for stylistic dating of the Spurlock mummy. Unfortunately, our face portrait is too poorly preserved to speculate about the artist who painted it, and not enough complete mummies from known contexts exist to associate the style of the wrappings with any particular embalming guild.

While stylistic comparisons point to a date of about A.D. 100 for the Spurlock mummy, it is unlikely that the specific provenance (particular tomb or site) will ever be known. The identification of the person inside the wrappings is equally uncertain. However, given the mixed population of the Fayum in Roman times, it is certainly possible that he or she was a person of Egyptian or Greek rather than Roman descent. In any case, it is clear that our mummy was no peasant. The lavish exterior, with its Roman-style face portrait and colored stucco surface highlighted with gold leaf, points to a high-status family that could afford one of the better mummification treatments for the period.

FIGURE 9 Manchester Museum mummy 1775 (Courtesy Manchester Museum, University of Manchester)

FIGURE 10 J. Paul Getty Museum mummy, probably from el-Hibeh (Courtesy J. Paul Getty Museum, Malibu, California. © The J. Paul Getty Museum)

4

IMAGING THE MUMMY

RADIOGRAPHY WAS THE FIRST STEP IN THE UNIVERSITY OF ILLINOIS
mummy examination because it was the best way to see the entire body
quickly and nondestructively. X rays provided important information on the
condition of the body and any objects wrapped up with it prior to using
more sophisticated techniques.

The mummy was X-rayed at the College of Veterinary Medicine by Richard Keen, a veterinary radiographer. It was laid on a table in a chamber
usually reserved for cows and horses. The group viewing the procedure
included veterinarians, a physical anthropologist, archaeologists, a dentist, and several interested students (figure 11).

The Spurlock mummy received fourteen X rays along its full length. One
veterinarian noticed that the jaw was angled to one side, indicating a
possible fracture (figure 12). The dentist pointed out baby teeth still in
place, with adult teeth coming in nearby. The arms were stretched out with
the hands resting on top of the thighs—a position sometimes associated
with male mummies (figure 13). The hands covered most of the genital
area, making it impossible to determine the sex of the person. No amulets or jewelry were visible, but this was not surprising in a Roman-period
mummy. Nor were there any obvious organ packages, indicating that some
organs might still be in their original positions. Dense areas inside the

abdomen seemed to confirm this, and observers speculated that heart and lungs might show up in a CT scan. A final observation was that especially dense patches—appearing white on the X ray—were probably gold leaf decorations visible on the outside of the mummy.

Linda Klepinger, a physical anthropologist with forensic experience, noticed that the epiphyses (growth plates at the ends of the long bones) at the wrists, hips, and knees were not fused (figure 14). This observation confirmed her earlier hunch, formed when examining loose foot bones, that the individual inside the wrappings was not an adult. The unfused growth plates, the appearance of the metatarsal bones, and the evidence of the teeth all indicated that our mummy was a child, about seven to nine years old at the time of death. This discovery explained why the mummy was so short—barely over four feet. The young age also explained why the shape of the pelvic bones could not be used to determine the child's sex.

Our more experienced radiographers pointed out rib fractures, especially on the lower right side, showing damage to the body before wrapping (or possibly caused by wrapping too tightly). Klepinger also noted a

FIGURE 11 Group of students and staff viewing the Spurlock mummy (Courtesy College of Veterinary Medicine, UIUC)

THE VIRTUAL MUMMY

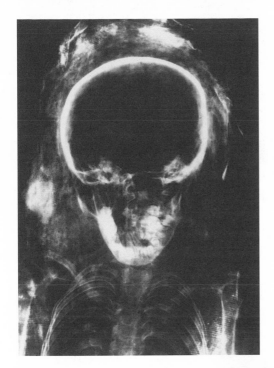

FIGURE 12 X ray of Spurlock mummy's skull (Courtesy R. Keen, College of Veterinary Medicine, UIUC)

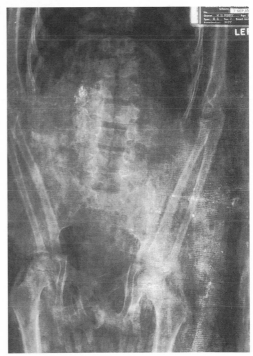

FIGURE 13 X ray of Spurlock mummy's torso and hands (Courtesy R. Keen, College of Veterinary Medicine, UIUC)

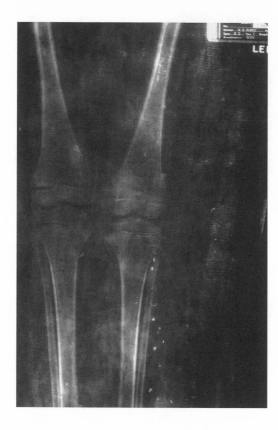

FIGURE 14 X ray of Spurlock mummy's legs (Courtesy R. Keen, College of Veterinary Medicine, UIUC)

lack of Harris lines—growth arrest lines in the long bones—that might have marked previous periods of malnutrition or sickness. There also was no radiographic evidence of chronic disease.

COMPUTERIZED TOMOGRAPHY (CT SCANNING)

CT scanning is another common medical diagnostic technique, especially useful for imaging soft-tissue injuries. It provides slices (cross sections rather like hardboiled egg slices) so that investigators can visually separate different layers instead of viewing them all at once. These slices are useful for studying aspects of mummification such as organ removal and methods of packing and wrapping. CT scans also provide the data used by increasingly sophisticated computer programs for three-dimensional reconstruction.

CT scanning was first used on Egyptian mummies during the 1970s. The Minneapolis Institute of Art scanned the mummy of Lady Teshat to investigate a second skull that had shown up on an X ray. The scans in Minneapolis (and later at the Mayo Clinic) showed several broken bones and creases on the bottoms of the feet. The team concluded that Teshat had been rewrapped in antiquity and that the second skull (from a different adult and another burial) had been inserted between her legs at that time.

Two sets of CT scans were performed on the Spurlock mummy, the first at Covenant Medical Center in Champaign, Illinois, and the second at Carle Clinic in Urbana, Illinois (figure 15). The first scan was a scout scan (a preliminary scan, to identify major features) at 10 mm intervals for the body, followed by 5 mm intervals for the head. The second set of scans imaged the head at 3 mm intervals in order to increase our chances for a successful 3-D reconstruction.

Immediately, there was new information that helped us interpret the X rays we had already examined. Layers of white (presumably hardened embalming fluids) appeared between layers of cloth wrappings. Other packing (mud or sawdust?) could not be identified. The jaw was not fractured but was tilted to one side as it rested on the mummy's chest (figure 16). Brain tissue was clearly present inside the skull and appeared to have different textures in different CT slices (figure 17).

Inside the thoracic cavity, rib fractures were confirmed, and we saw for the first time that the chest was collapsed (figure 18). Joseph Barkmeier, a Carle radiologist, could see the brain, heart, and lungs still in place, although he noted they were "all dried up and moved around"—not in their usual places.

Shriveled-up eyeballs were visible, as was at least one fracture on the lower back part of the skull. Was this the cause of death? Barkmeier thought this was probably not the case. To him, the fractures looked more like postmortem breaks since he could not detect any pooled blood. He added that the two densities of brain tissue seen in some of the CT slices were probably two parts of the brain: cerebrum and cerebellum. Clearly the embalmers had not removed the brain through the bone at the back of the nose as in many earlier mummies.

The most surprising discovery was a wooden board that ran under the full length of the mummy inside the wrappings. The wood grain was quite

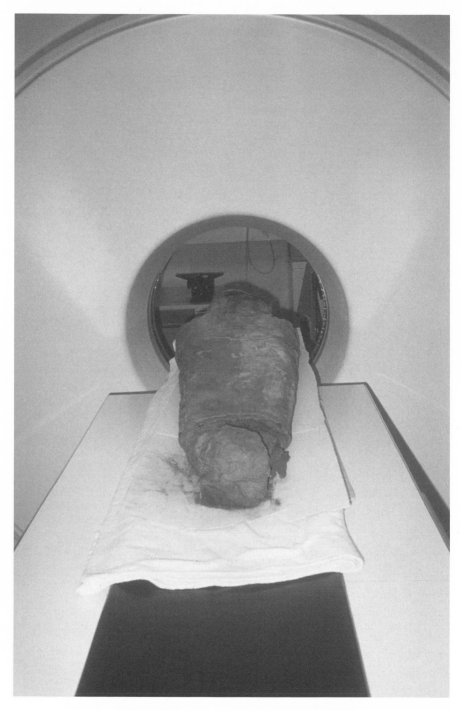

FIGURE 15 Mummy going into CT scanner at Carle Clinic (Courtesy S. Wisseman)

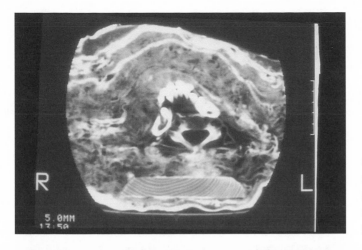

FIGURE 16 CT slice, mummy's jaw (Courtesy Carle Clinic, Urbana, Illinois)

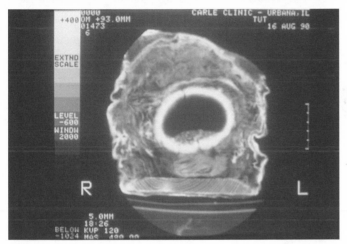

FIGURE 17 CT slice, mummy's brain (Courtesy Carle Clinic, Urbana, Illinois)

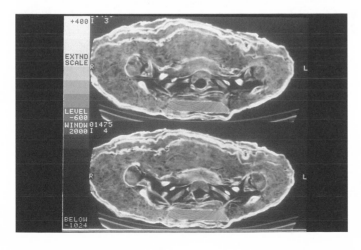

FIGURE 18 CT slices, mummy's collapsed chest (Courtesy Carle Clinic, Urbana, Illinois)

visible, and we could count some of the rings (not enough to date the board by dendrochronology, since the board is far from being the full cross section of a tree). The edges of the board were beveled, indicating some care in its preparation.

How did we miss this board in the X rays? When we checked the X rays again, it appeared in a few faint lines at the lower end of the mummy (figure 19). Most of the board was hidden by layers of bone and wrappings. Several people noticed that the width of the board changed as the CT scanner moved down the body; possibly there was more than one board under our mummy as in one of the mummies from the Museum of Fine Arts in Boston.

Details of the embalming process began to emerge: extra rolls of linen placed under the fractured skull, additional packing over the chest (probably to puff it out and make the mummy appear more lifelike), and separate wrapping of the hands (figure 20) just like the Ptolemaic period mummy in Indianapolis. Unfortunately, the sex remained an open question; we still do not know if our mummy is a boy or a girl.

FIGURE 19 X ray of Spurlock mummy's lower legs (Courtesy R. Keen, College of Veterinary Medicine, UIUC)

PLATE 1 Spurlock Museum mummy, detail of lower end (Courtesy S. Wisseman)

PLATE 2 Spurlock Museum mummy, detail of face portrait (Courtesy S. Wisseman)

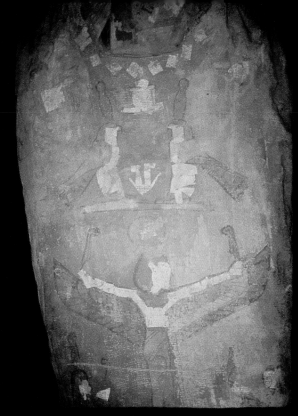

PLATE 3 Spurlock Museum mummy, detail of *wadjet* (eyes), Horus falcons, and Nut (Courtesy S. Wisseman)

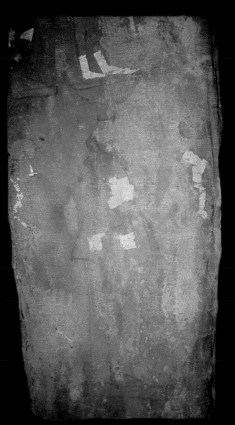

PLATE 4 Spurlock Museum mummy, detail of Osiris (Courtesy S. Wisseman)

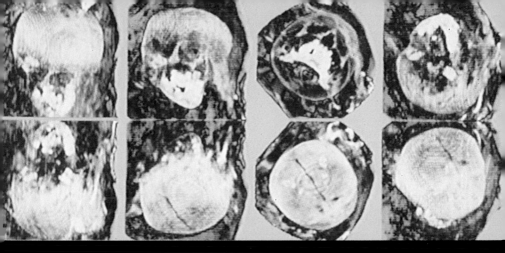

PLATE 5 Volumetric rendering of "tumbling skull" (Courtesy D. Lawrance, National Center for Supercomputing Applications, UIUC)

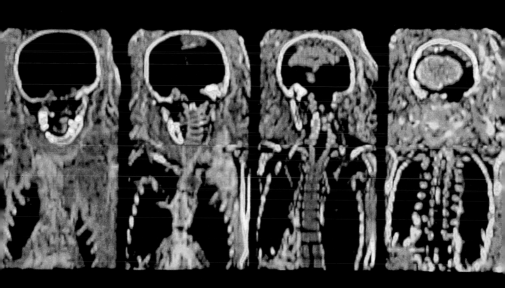

PLATE 6 Volumetric rendering of mummy's torso (Courtesy D. Lawrance, National

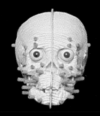 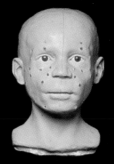 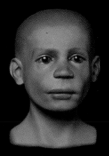

PLATE 7 Stages in the construction of the mummy sculpture (Courtesy R. Evenhouse, School of Biomedical and Health Information Sciences, University of Illinois at Chicago)

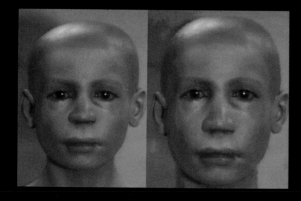

PLATE 8 Aging our mummy to age eighteen (Courtesy R. Evenhouse, School of Biomedical and Health Information Sciences, University of Illinois at Chicago)

PLATE 9 Stereolithography skull (Courtesy R. Evenhouse, School of Biomedical and Health Information Sciences, University of Illinois at Chicago)

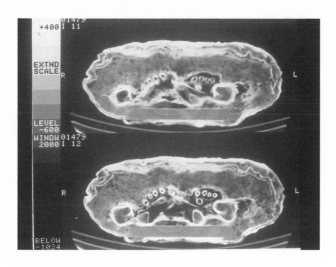

FIGURE 20 CT slices, Spurlock mummy's hands (Courtesy Carle Clinic, Urbana, Illinois)

THREE-DIMENSIONAL RECONSTRUCTION

Armed with the CT scan data, the team went to the National Center for Supercomputing Applications (NCSA) at the University of Illinois to attempt three-dimensional reconstructions of the mummy's head. Such reconstructions had been performed before on Egyptian mummies in museum collections in Boston, Indianapolis, and parts of Europe, but never with a Cray II supercomputer. Most of these earlier reconstructions were based on accurate measurements of the body taken from the surfaces of completely unwrapped mummies. In our case, since the body was still covered in many layers of cloth, the dimensions of bone and any remaining tissue would be taken from the highest resolution CT scan images we could obtain.

The CT scans were subjected to two types of three-dimensional imaging. The first was a program (Viewit) written by Clinton Potter and Rachael Brady of NCSA and used by David Lawrance. The software uses volumetric rendering, a technique that does not rely upon the prior identification of surfaces but renders all volume elements (voxels) as semitransparent masses—sort of like cubes of jello. The program was a good choice for a wrapped mummy with inaccessible body surfaces. Even with a supercomputer, however, it was not possible to see everything through the dense layers of resin-impregnated wrappings, stucco, paint, and gold leaf.

The results, translated into high-quality videos, were exciting. It was like doing a virtual autopsy by computer—layers were stripped off one by one, and everything could be rotated on a computer screen without moving or harming the actual mummy. Particularly interesting were views dubbed the "tumbling skull" (the head rotating in space, end over end) that showed the child's open growth suture on the top of the skull, the complete jaw with no distortion, and an aberrant tooth (plate 5). Was this a loose tooth, like the one found lodged in the pharynx of the mummy of the Nineteenth Dynasty pharaoh Merneptah? A local orthodontist, Morgan Powell, thought it more likely to be an unerupted bicuspid tooth—something he was used to seeing in modern children.

Cutaway views made it possible to look inside the skull and observe the shrunken brain tissue from several angles and to examine the back of the skull for the first time. From the side, it was clear that our child's jaw had significant prognathism—protrusion of the lower part of the face. Heart and lungs in the thoracic cavity were more visible than in any of the previous images (plate 6).

Finally, the computer stripped away the body itself, revealing the surface of the board for the first time (figure 21). Not only was there distinct

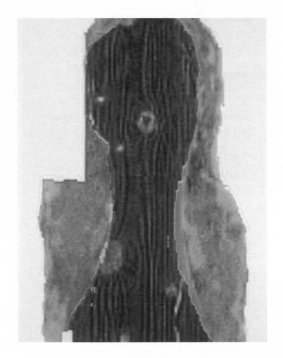

FIGURE 21 Volumetric rendering of wooden board (Courtesy D. Lawrance, National Center for Supercomputing Applications, UIUC)

wood grain, but we could see a large knothole. Now it was clear that only one board was present and that it had an unusual shape: wide under the head, narrow under the neck, and wide again under the torso. Was this a recycled board from another use, or had the embalmers deliberately shaped the wood to fit the body? Such a procedure would be unusual, especially during the Roman period when embalmers tended to simplify mummification by skipping evisceration and removal of the brain.

The second 3-D rendering of the CT scan slices was a sculpture. David Lawrance had recommended Raymond Evenhouse, a biomedical illustrator at the University of Illinois at Chicago, for his work on mummies in the Indianapolis Children's Museum and the Kalamazoo Public Museum. Evenhouse jumped at the chance to make a reconstructed head in time for the World Heritage Museum's exhibit *Bound for Eternity*.

Evenhouse laboriously converted each two-dimensional CT film of the head into a Styrofoam slice. Then he stacked these slices up to form the basis for his three-dimensional sculpture (figure 22). Instead of using mea-

FIGURE 22 CT slices converted to Styrofoam (Courtesy R. Evenhouse, School of Biomedical and Health Information Sciences, University of Illinois at Chicago)

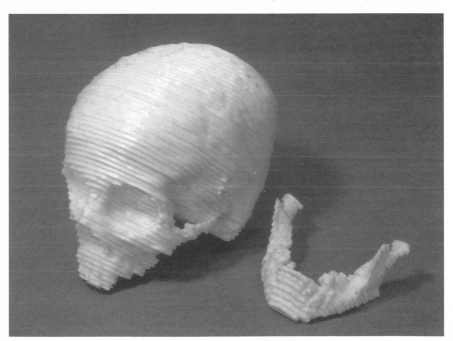

surements of dead bodies to approximate tissue depth, which results in lifeless-looking reconstructions, he used a profile sketch and blue tissue markers based on ultrasound and X-ray data from live people of different ages and backgrounds. He literally "put the flesh back on the bones," adding modeling clay up to the depth of the markers and using his "best approximations"—averages based on the shape of the rest of the face—for the ears and nose. The final head, cast in plastic, was tinted a light brown because of the prognathism and other facial characteristics that suggested a child of mixed race (plate 7). Using special software, Evenhouse also projected our mummy into the future, resulting in an image of what he or she would have looked like at the age of eighteen (plate 8).

Later, when Evenhouse changed jobs and moved to MicroCut Engineering, he was able to redo the Spurlock mummy head using stereolithography. He fed digitized CT data into a computer-aided design (CAD) program that controlled a laser beam, causing the skull to rise magically out of a vat of liquid polymer (plate 9). This technique is both more accurate and much faster than the earlier method Evenhouse used to make a head for the museum exhibit.

5

PHYSICAL REMAINS AND

EMBALMING METHODS

PREVIOUS MUMMY PROJECTS, ESPECIALLY THOSE AT MANCHESTER University and the University of Pennsylvania, have succeeded in extracting a great deal of information from the wrappings and embalming materials used in Egyptian mummies. In both cases, however, destructive autopsies were used to take samples.

In the Illinois project, we were fortunate in that the wrappings around the lower end of the mummy were loose, releasing bits of cloth, bone, dried resin, and even insects. These could be examined without doing any damage to the main mummy, and they provided a golden opportunity for us to investigate Roman-period mummification methods.

THE WOODEN BOARD

Our biggest surprise in CT scans was the sudden appearance of a wooden board underneath the head of the mummy. What was the purpose of this board? Was it a "stiffening" surface, used to support a decaying or imperfectly preserved corpse? How common was the practice in other mummies of the Roman period? A search of the literature uncovered several examples of boards in other late mummies, including Manchester Museum 1768 and 9313, Pennsylvania University Museum IV, and two mummies in the Boston Museum of Fine Arts. Three of these mummies exhibit evidence of either poor condition prior to embalming (e.g., insect damage) or mishandling (postmortem fracturing due to careless transporting or stacking of the body, or perhaps applying wrappings too tightly). Other examples of wooden supports probably exist, but as we had discovered, the faint outlines of a board underneath multiple layers of wrappings and bones are hard to detect in an X ray unless one is carefully looking for them. Reexamination of existing X rays for other Roman mummies of this period will probably produce more examples of boards.

After we knew what to look for, we returned to the Spurlock mummy and found an exposed corner of the board near the edge of already loosened wrappings.

The type of wood used might tell us something about the economy of mummification in Roman Egypt: was the wood a native species, or was it imported? A sliver of the wood was taken to Stanley Ambrose in the Department of Anthropology. Ambrose guessed it was cedar from the aroma of the wood, but he suggested that he mail it to a friend in Brussels who was an expert in African wood species. Roger DeChamps of the Musée Royal de L'Afrique Centrale obliged with some scanning electron micrographs and an identification of *Cedrus atlantica*—a type of cedar common in Morocco and North Africa (figure 23). This means that the Egyptian embalmers did not have to rely on cedar imported all the way from Lebanon but could (and did) obtain the wood for such boards, as well as for coffins, closer to home.

ATAM then recruited Dennis Coleman and Jack Liu of the Illinois State Geological Survey for radiocarbon dating. This method uses organic, carbon-containing materials to measure the amount of the carbon isotope ^{14}C remaining in the sample. This radioactive isotope, generated in the atmosphere by the interaction of cosmic rays with carbon dioxide, is absorbed by all living plants and animals. When the organism dies, absorption stops, and the isotope decays at a known rate.

Since the exposed corner of the board could be sampled without damage to the rest of the mummy, the museum gave us permission to go ahead. The wood was surprisingly difficult to sample. It was as hard as rock, probably from the hardening over time of a large quantity of resin and other substances used by the embalmers (the hardened embalming fluids

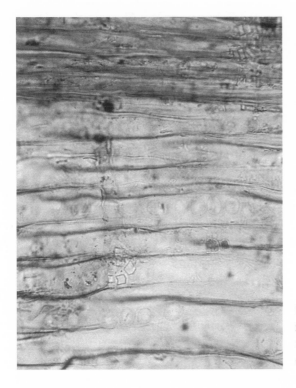

FIGURE 23 Micrograph of wood sample (Courtesy R. DeChamps)

may also explain the inordinate heaviness of the mummy despite its small size). Coleman and Liu realized that they would have to strip the sample of embalming fluids before the ^{14}C test could be run.

The result of the ^{14}C test was a conventional date of 2140 radiocarbon years before present (B.P.), plus or minus 160 years, calibrated to approximately 190 B.C. with a similar margin of error. Even the later end of this time span is earlier than the stylistic date of about A.D. 100, obtained from the style of the Roman face portrait and the gilded and painted zones of Egyptian gods on the surface of the mummy. Part of the explanation may be that the tree from which the board was taken was cut down many years before the mummy was embalmed (the radiocarbon clock starts when the tree dies). Then the board itself was probably recycled, since wood was precious in ancient Egypt and would not have been discarded without good reason. The other possible explanation was that the embalming fluids contained bitumen, a petroleum derivative with ancient carbon in it. A bitumen soaking would affect the ^{14}C date by making the board appear to be older than it really was.

ATAM staff used tweezers to collect about 100 mg of hardened resin, which resembled bits of smoky glass, from inside the loosened wrappings at the mummy's ankles. The sample was then turned over to Kenneth Rinehart and Mark Proefke in the Department of Chemistry.

We know from ancient historians such as Herodotus that Egyptian embalmers used a variety of substances to preserve the surface of the body after the viscera had been removed and the tissues desiccated. These included Chios turpentine (terebinth), mastic, pine pitch, gum resins such as frankincense and myrrh, beeswax and plant waxes, and bitumen (a type of asphalt or petroleum derivative). The name "mummy" comes from the Persian word *mummia,* meaning "bitumen" or "bitumenous thing," because the dried and hardened resins looked like bitumen. However, other studies have shown that bitumen was used only sporadically in the embalming of Egyptian mummies.

The chemists told us that even armed with the above information on embalming fluids, their task would not be easy. The separation and identification of these various substances after so long a time lapse was quite difficult and time-consuming. Our sample was messy, consisting of small, hard pieces of uneven brown color mixed with bits of fabric, sand, and other inorganic materials. Proefke and Rinehart simplified the analysis by first separating the resin sample into acidic and neutral parts. This involved a complicated sequence of steps, beginning with dissolving the resin in chloroform. Two techniques were used at this stage, gas chromatography mass spectrometry (GC/MS) and fast atom bombardment tandem mass spectrometry (FABMS).

The results revealed three compounds in the resins, all forms of abietic acid (figure 24). Since abietic acid is found in nearly all naturally occurring coniferous resins, these compounds firmly identify the material as a pine pitch and are very similar to those in resins found in other archaeological samples from the Mediterranean. So we were able to say pine pitch was used, but it was not possible to determine which specific kind of tree was the source of the resin.

Unlike the resin in Manchester Museum mummy 1770, our resin did not appear to contain plant or insect waxes. However, the chemists noted that

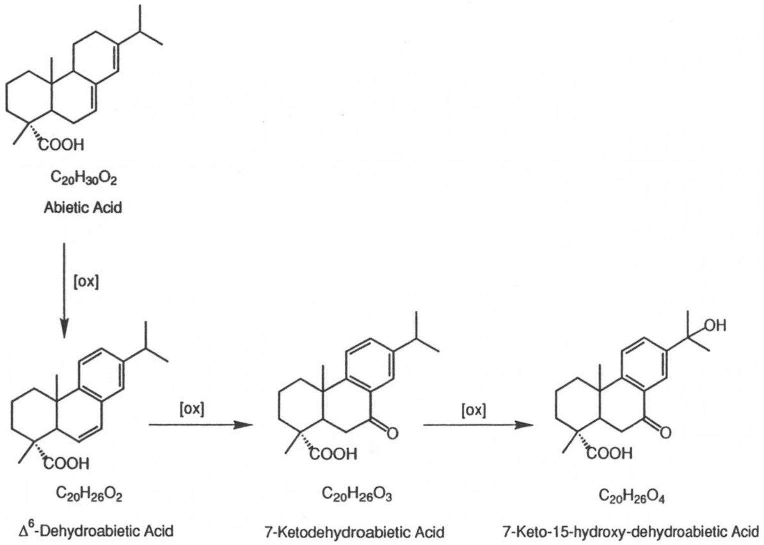

FIGURE 24 Oxidation products of abietic acid found in the mummy resin (Courtesy M. Proefke and K. Rinehart, Chemistry, UIUC)

the hydrocarbon chain lengths found in the first tests were consistent with some bitumen being present. They confirmed this by a third test, trace metal analysis by plasma atomic emission spectroscopy, which identified three metals characteristic of petroleum: vanadium, nickel, and molybdenum (figure 25). This bitumen was similar to reported Dead Sea and Mesopotamian bitumen used in Ptolemaic mummies. The test also explained the early radiocarbon date on our mummy as the result of the board's being impregnated with a substance—bitumen—with much older carbon than the wood itself.

FLESH-EATING INSECTS

Another test was a spinoff from the resin analysis. While collecting bits of hardened resin, our team (figure 26) encountered several dried-up carcasses of insects. The most complete insect was turned over to Eli Levine in the Illinois State Natural History Survey, who gave it to a beetle specialist, John Bouseman. Bouseman examined the insect under the microscope and concluded that it was probably *Necrobia rupifes,* a type of beetle that feasts on decaying flesh. This was the same type of beetle found in one

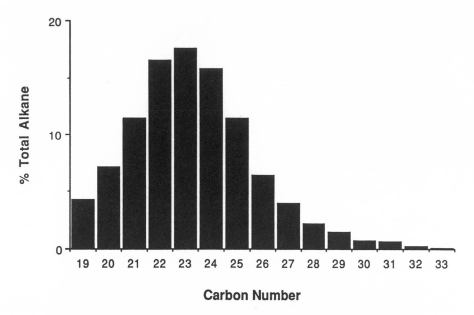

FIGURE 25 Distribution of *n*-alkanes found in the mummy resin (Courtesy M. Proefke and K. Rinehart, Chemistry, UIUC)

FIGURE 26 UIUC mummy project, chemistry team; left to right: Kenneth Rinehart, Sarah Wisseman, Mark Proefke, Mastura Raheel, Stanley Ambrose (Courtesy B. Wiegand, UIUC News Bureau)

of the Manchester Museum mummies. Bouseman noted that our speci-
men was certainly old because it had no *setae* (hairs) left. Finding this sort
of beetle, rather than the kind that infests museum storage areas, supports
the idea that the body was not in pristine condition when the embalming
procedures were initiated. In fact, our mummy may have been in the same
state of decay as its closest parallel in terms of age, date, and number of
organs present: Pennsylvania University Museum mummy IV.

TEXTILE ANALYSIS

Now that we had information on the embalming fluids, we were curious
about the nature of the fabric used to wrap the mummy. We asked Mastura Raheel, a textile chemist in the Division of Consumer Sciences, to help.
Linen cloth, made from flax fibers, was the most common fabric used, but
various sources report other fabrics such as ramie and possibly cotton.

Raheel used both optical and scanning electron microscopy to examine our mummy wrappings. She discovered that fabrics of three distinctly
different weights were used. The outermost fabric was the heaviest of the
three, while the innermost layer was the lightest and most densely woven
(figures 27–28). All three fabrics were plain-woven structures of light beige
to brown color. Since it appeared that the color was due to the embalming fluids and natural aging of the fibers, dye analysis was not undertak-
en. Raheel characterized each fabric by weight, yarn size, yarn twist, and
fiber diameter. Then she prepared selected fibers for scanning electron
microscopy (SEM), which involved removing dirt and dried resins using a
soaking and shaking procedure. Some of the fibers were so brittle that they
ruptured during preparation.

SEM revealed the thick walls, nodes (swollen joints), and crosswise
beat marks characteristic of flax in the two innermost layers of wrappings
(figure 29). The beat marks were caused when the stalks of flax were ret-
ted (rotted) and then beaten in order to remove the woody covering and
obtain the fiber. The cross sections of these fibers showed the thick walls,
small lumen, and rounded polygonal shape of flax (figure 30).

In the outermost fabric wrapping, Raheel found crossmarks but no nodes
as in flax (figure 31). Also, the cross section showed an oval or bean-shaped
structure with an elliptical lumen—a characteristic of ramie (figure 32). It

FIGURE 27 Ramie wrappings (Courtesy M. Raheel, Textile Science, UIUC)

FIGURE 28 Linen wrappings (Courtesy M. Raheel, Textile Science, UIUC)

FIGURE 29 Flax fibers, longitudinal view (Courtesy M. Raheel, Textile Science, UIUC)

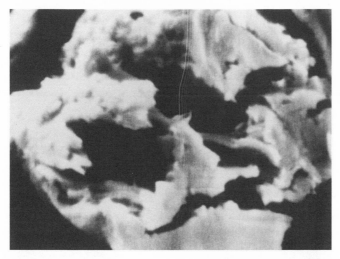

FIGURE 30 Flax fiber, cross section (Courtesy M. Raheel, Textile Science, UIUC)

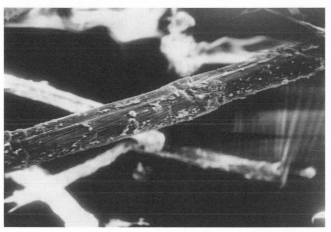

FIGURE 31 Ramie fibers, longitudinal view (Courtesy M. Raheel, Textile Science, UIUC)

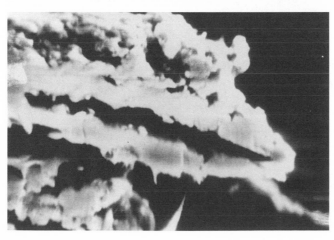

FIGURE 32 Ramie fiber, cross section (Courtesy M. Raheel, Textile Science, UIUC)

was difficult to be certain that our sample was ramie because immature flax fibers can also have large lumens; however, we know that ramie was used during the Roman period in Egypt. Ramie contains non-fibrous matter that is toxic to bacteria and fungi; possibly the Egyptians knew this and deliberately chose ramie as the protective outer wrapping for mummies.

BONE ANALYSIS

In addition to bits of wood, hardened resin, and insect carcasses, the loosened wrappings at the foot of our mummy also contained loose foot bones. One was given to Stanley Ambrose to attempt a reconstruction of the child's diet using stable isotope analysis. The technique is based upon the fact that C_4 plants (for example, maize and sorghum) use different enzymes to fix atmospheric carbon than do C_3 plants (wheat, rice, fruits, and nuts). Carbon preserved in the mineral phase of bone (carbonate) reflects carbohydrate consumption from the different plant groups in the form of distinct ratios of two carbon isotopes, ^{13}C and ^{12}C. The difference between carbon isotope ratios of carbonate and the organic phase of bone (collagen) can reflect isotopically different sources for protein and energy components of the diet.

The mummy's "collagen" turned out to be non-collagenous. It was badly degraded and possibly contaminated by embalming fluids. Nevertheless, the carbonate carbon ratios are close to those expected for a typical Egyptian diet with carbohydrate staples of bread and onions (C_3 foods).

OTHER TESTS

A small sample of mummy tissue was sent by Barbara Bohen to a Danish team of DNA researchers who volunteered to identify the mummy's sex using ancient DNA. Although DNA was found, the sex could not be determined because the sample was cloudy—perhaps due to contamination with embalming fluids.

A final series of tests was performed on the red, stucco-like surface of the mummy to determine the composition of the plaster and of the red pigment used to color it. A. Eades, A. Kahn, and R. Haasch of the Materials Research Laboratory used a combination of proton-induced X-ray emission (PIXE), Rutherford backscattering (RBS), and X-ray photoelectron spectroscopy (XPS) (figure 33). The results showed a typical gypsum-based plaster (hydrous calcium sulfate, $CaSO_4 \cdot 2H_2O$). The red of the pigment is probably a lead oxide, red lead or Pb_3O_4.

FIGURE 33 XPS analysis of mummy stucco (Courtesy R. Haasch, Materials Research Laboratory, UIUC)

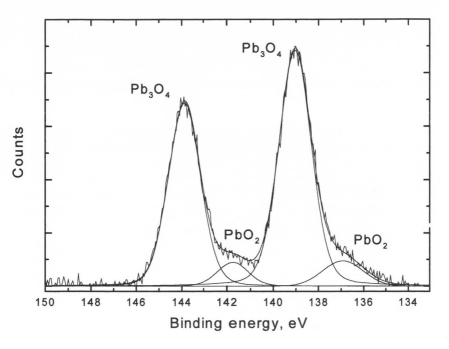

PHYSICAL REMAINS AND EMBALMING METHODS

THE SPURLOCK MUMMY
AND THE FUTURE OF
MUMMY STUDIES

THE UNIVERSITY OF ILLINOIS MUMMY PROJECT IS NOW ON RECORD as one of many scientific investigations of ancient Egyptian mummies. Our findings have been shared with scholars in England and Minnesota who maintain databases on mummies (Rosalie David's database on Egyptian mummies in Manchester, England, and Arthur Aufderheide's database on mummies from many parts of the world at the University of Minnesota at Duluth).

Our mummy project differed from the major studies conducted in the 1970s (Manchester and Philadelphia) in that our methods were nondestructive. Most of our information was gathered using the noninvasive imaging techniques of radiography and CT scanning. The sampling of tiny amounts of wood, stucco, cloth, and resin collected from the lower end of the mummy for dating and compositional analyses did not detract from its display quality. Although our mummy was never autopsied, we managed to extract considerable information about the body inside the wrappings and about the mummification procedures.

From the X rays and CT scans, we confirmed that our mummy was not an adult but a seven-to-nine-year-old child of unknown sex. He or she had several fractures of the lower skull and ribs, probably acquired after death. The child was mummified with his internal organs left in place and the tissues already under attack by necrobic beetles. A wooden "stiffening board" supported the broken head and decaying flesh and was wrapped up with the body. This board may have been used initially either to move the body or to serve as a work surface in the embalming facility.

The embalmers took special care of the Spurlock child once they began their treatment. The broken head was cradled in extra rolled cloth, and the hands were separately wrapped. Sufficient packing material (cloth, and possibly mud or sawdust) was used to pad out the body and make it appear lifelike. Multiple layers of linen and ramie were used to wrap the body, separated by liquid resin that permeated everything and added to the final weight of the mummy.

The features of the Spurlock mummy are best paralleled in PUM IV, the mummy of a young child housed in the University Museum, University of Pennsylvania. Like our mummy, PUM IV was in a state of advanced decay and was wrapped with a full-length board underneath. X rays showed occipital skull fractures, probably from postmortem damage, no Harris lines indicating prolonged periods of malnutrition or disease, open epiphyses, and several unerupted teeth. PUM IV (a boy) was probably about eight years old at the time of death—just like the Spurlock mummy. A full autopsy revealed that PUM IV had numerous insect larvae and scarab beetles, no recognizable organs left, and large masses of packing, possibly sawdust. The conclusion reached by the autopsy team was that PUM IV had probably been eviscerated by a corrosive enema administered through the anus (the second method of embalming described by Herodotus), and that the mummy dated to the first century A.D.

The two facial reconstructions based on the Carle Clinic CT scans provided some additional information about the child's ancestry. The prognathism of the lower face was a Negroid feature, suggesting a child of mixed race. Since intermarriage among Egyptians, Greeks, and Romans was common during the Roman period and the Fayum was a melting pot of settlers from all over the Mediterranean as well as other parts of Africa during this period, this conclusion was not unreasonable.

The combined evidence of the physical remains, the embalming techniques, and the gilded and painted surface indicated that our child came from a good family—one with the financial means to afford one of the better mummies of the Roman period. The lack of Harris lines on the long bones shows that he did not experience long periods of disease or mal-nutrition. He could, however, have died from a quick hit-and-run illness that left no trace on the skeleton.

A death from a sudden, virulent illness (for example, an epidemic) at a time when many other people were sick and dying could explain why the child's body did not receive immediate attention. The local embalmers might have had a backlog of corpses to deal with, so the child's body was allowed to decay partially before it was treated.

The other explanation for poor preservation and the presence of flesh-eating beetles is simply that the embalming job was insufficient to halt decay. Necrobic beetles have been found in other mummies of this peri-od (such as PUM IV), supporting the historical accounts that embalmers during the Roman period focused their attention on the external appear-ance of their mummies rather than halting decay and preserving tissues.

The Spurlock mummy is only one of many Egyptian mummies that have been studied using both nondestructive and destructive techniques. It fits well with other mummies that display the considerable variation in mum-mification techniques and wrapping styles typical of the Roman period. As in PUM IV, our child's brain was left in place. A "stiffening board" was used, just as in two mummies in the Boston Museum of Fine Arts and in Manchester Museum mummy 1768. The Spurlock mummy displays regis-ters of Egyptian gods on the exterior front, like Manchester Museum mum-my 1775 but unlike another in the British Museum (London) that is wrapped with bandages in an elaborate criss-cross pattern.

Where will mummy studies go from here? For some investigators, like Bob Brier of Long Island University, there is the experimental mummifica-tion route. In 1994, Brier reconstructed the complete Egyptian embalming process, using the body of an anonymous seventy-six-year-old man who had died of a heart attack. His team followed the description by Herodo-tus as closely as possible: the brain was removed with a hook, the viscera were extracted using an obsidian blade, and the body was dried for thirty-five days under a large pile of natron. The result was a well-preserved mummy, now stored in a temperature-controlled chamber at the Univer-sity of Maryland Medical School in Baltimore. Brier's efforts were docu-mented in a television special.

Although such an experiment generates valuable information about aspects of embalming (such as how long it really takes and how much natron is required to do a good job), most museum curators prefer a less messy, hands-off approach to mummy research. The most promising avenue is the increasingly sophisticated imaging technology available through hospitals and universities. X rays and CT scans are much higher resolution than even a decade ago, and advances in computer software make better three-dimensional reconstructions than was possible when our project was conducted in the early 1990s. Just recently, the Austrian Iceman was X-rayed again, this time with one of the newer instruments, and a startling new find was made: the Iceman had an arrowhead buried in his torso, indicating that he died from murder rather than simple exposure.

Some portable instruments, such as the X-ray equipment of the Quinnipiac University Bioanthropology Research Institute, in Hamden, Connecticut, allow researchers to visit museums instead of transporting mummies to hospitals. This is a distinct advantage in terms of artifact preservation, and curators are much more likely to give permission for imaging when it can be done both nondestructively and in situ. Finally, the advances in Web-based databases mean that both two-dimensional and three-dimensional images can be shared over the Internet (for example, North Dakota State University has an Archaeology Technologies laboratory that is archiving 3-D models of artifacts). When Egyptian mummy X rays and CT scans are digitized and made available to researchers all over the world using this medium, it will be much easier to explore the full range of variation in mummification practices over time.

APPENDIX

A CHRONOLOGY OF ANCIENT EGYPT

Archaic Period	Dynasties 1–2	(3050–2663 B.C.)
Old Kingdom	Dynasties 3–6	(2663–2195 B.C.)
First Intermediate Period	Dynasties 7/8–11a	(2195–2066 B.C.)
Middle Kingdom	Dynasties 11b-13	(2066–1650 B.C.)
Second Intermediate Period	Dynasties 15–17	(1650–1549 B.C.)
New Kingdom	Dynasties 18–20	(1549–1069 B.C.)
Third Intermediate Period	Dynasties 21–25	(1064–656 B.C.)
Saite Period	Dynasty 26	(664–525 B.C.)
Late Period	Dynasties 27–31	(525–332 B.C.)
Hellenistic Period		(332–30 B.C.)
Roman Period		(30 B.C.–A.D. 395)
Byzantine Period		(A.D. 395–640)
Arab Period		(A.D. 640–1517)

SOURCE: After Ikram and Dodson, *The Mummy in Ancient Egypt.*

ANNOTATED BIBLIOGRAPHY

GENERAL BOOKS ON EGYPT

Bowman, Alan K. *Egypt after the Pharaohs, 332* B.C.–A.D. *642*. Berkeley: University of California Press, 1989.

Brewer, Douglas J., and Emily Teeter. *Egypt and the Egyptians*. Cambridge: Cambridge University Press, 1999.

Hobson, Christine. *The World of the Pharaohs*. New York: Thames and Hudson, 1991.

James, T. G. H. *An Introduction to Ancient Egypt*. New York: Harper and Row, 1979.

GENERAL BOOKS ON MUMMIES

Adams, Barbara. *Egyptian Mummies*. 2d ed. Aylesbury, Eng.: Shire Publications, 1988.

Andrews, Carol. *Egyptian Mummies*. Cambridge, Mass.: Harvard University Press, 1984. Well-illustrated general account featuring mummies in the British Museum.

Dunand, Françoise, and Roger Lichtenberg. *Mummies: A Voyage through Eternity*. New York: Abrams, 1991.

El Mahdy, Christine. *Mummies, Myth and Magic*. New York: Thames and Hudson, 1989. Lively and useful account of the history of mummies and early investigations.

Ikram, Salima, and Aidan Dodson. *The Mummy in Ancient Egypt: Equipping the Dead for Eternity*. London: Thames and Hudson, 1998. Extensively researched, detailed, and up-to-date account.

Smith, G. Elliott, and Warren R. Dawson. *Egyptian Mummies*. London: Kegan Paul, 1924. Reprint, 1991.

Spencer, A. J. *Death in Ancient Egypt*. New York: Penguin Books, 1982.

MUMMY PORTRAITS

Bagnall, R. S. "The Fayum and Its People." In *Ancient Faces: Mummy Portraits from Roman Egypt,* ed. Susan Walker, 26–29. New York: Metropolitan Museum of Art and Routledge, 2000. Useful description of the melting-pot nature of the Fayum region.

Doxiadis, Euphrosyne. *The Mysterious Fayum Portraits: Faces from Ancient Egypt.* London: Thames and Hudson, 1995.

Thompson, David L. *Mummy Portraits at the J. Paul Getty Museum.* Malibu, Calif.: J. Paul Getty Museum, 1976. Excellent background on mummy portraits; well illustrated.

SCIENTIFIC STUDIES OF MUMMIES

Beckett, Ronald, Gerald Conlogue, and John Posh. "Picturing the Past: The Tools of Medicine Let Ancient Mummies Tell Their Tales." *Discovering Archaeology* (December 2000): 66–75.

Cockburn, Aidan, Eve Cockburn, and Theodore A. Reyman, eds. *Mummies, Disease and Ancient Cultures.* 2d ed. Cambridge: Cambridge University Press, 1998. Excellent background on mummy studies around the world.

David, A. R., ed. *Science in Egyptology.* Manchester, Eng.: Manchester University Press, 1986.

David, A. R., and R. Archbold. *Conversations with Mummies: New Light on the Lives of Ancient Egyptians.* New York: Madison Press, 2000. Best recent overview of studies of Egyptian mummies, lavishly illustrated and full of colorful details not found elsewhere.

David, A. Rosalie, ed. *The Manchester Museum Mummy Project.* Manchester, Eng.: Manchester University Press, 1979. Technical account with detailed photographs and X rays.

David, A. Rosalie, and Edmund Tapp. *Evidence Embalmed: Modern Medicine and the Mummies of Ancient Egypt.* Manchester, Eng.: Manchester University Press, 1984.

——, eds. *The Mummy's Tale: The Scientific and Medical Investigation of Natsef-Amun, Priest in the Temple at Karnak.* New York: St. Martin's, 1993.

Diener, L. "Radiology of Two Child-Mummies in Stockholm: Surprising Results." *MASCA Journal* 1, no. 7 (1981): 218–20. X rays reveal that "child" mummies contain bird skeletons.

Fleming, Stuart, Bernard Fishman, David O'Connor, and David Silverman. *The Egyptian Mummy: Secrets and Science.* Philadelphia: University Museum, University of Pennsylvania, 1980. Exhibit catalog, very detailed, with great micrographs of ancient parasites.

Germer, Renate. *Mummies: Life after Death in Ancient Egypt.* Munich: Prestel, 1997. Covers recent mummy research in Europe, especially Germany.

Hamner, James Edward, ed. *Se-Ankh: An Interdisciplinary Historical and Biomedical Study of an Egyptian Mummy Head.* Memphis: University of Tennessee, 1987.

Harris, James, and Kent Weeks. *X-ray Atlas of the Royal Mummies.* Chicago: University of Chicago Press, 1980. Technical account of the 1960s studies of mummies in the Cairo Museum.

———. *X-raying the Pharaohs.* New York: Scribner, 1973.

Haynes, Joyce, and R. Jackson Wilson. *Padihershef: The Egyptian Mummy.* Springfield, Mass.: George Walter Vincent Smith Art Museum, 1984.

Holt, Frank L. "Mystery Mummy." *Archaeology* (November–December 1991): 44–51.

Lupton, Carter. "Contribution of CT to the Understanding of Egyptian Mummification Technique." In *Proceedings of the First World Congress on Mummy Studies,* 515–22. Tenerife, Canary Islands: Museo Arqueologico y Etnologico, 1995.

———. "An Historical Study of Two Egyptian Mummies in the Milwaukee Public Museum." In *Human Remains: Conservation, Retrieval and Analysis,* ed. Emily Williams, 215–25. BAR International Series 934. Oxford: Archaeopress, 2001. Proceedings of a conference held in Williamsburg, Va., Nov. 7–11, 1999.

Magee, Reginald. "Arterial Disease in Antiquity." *Medical Journal of Australia* 169 (1998): 663–66. Technical account, featuring paleopathology of Egyptian mummies. Also available on-line (see below under "Web Resources").

Marx, Myron, and Sue H. D'Auria. "CT Examination of Eleven Egyptian Mummies." *RadioGraphics* 6, no. 2 (1986): 321–30. Imaging of mummies in the Boston Museum of Fine Arts.

Pettitt, Charles, and George Fildes. "The International Egyptian Mummy Data Base." In *Science in Egyptology,* ed. A. Rosalie David, 177–81. Manchester, Eng.: Manchester University Press, 1986.

Pringle, Heather. *The Mummy Congress: Science, Obsession, and the Everlasting Dead.* New York: Hyperion, 2001.

Reyman, Theodore A., and William H. Peck. "Egyptian Mummification with Evisceration per Ano." In *Mummies, Disease and Ancient Cultures,* ed. Aidan Cockburn, Eve Cockburn, and Theodore A. Reyman, 106–20. 2d ed. Cambridge: Cambridge University Press, 1998.

Taylor, John H. *Unwrapping a Mummy.* Austin: University of Texas Press, 1995. Thoroughly detailed account of the unwrapping, autopsy, and tissue studies of the mummy of an Egyptian priest named Horemkenesi.

THE UNIVERSITY OF ILLINOIS MUMMY

Bohen, Barbara. "Collaborative Investigation of the University of Illinois Egypto-Roman Mummy." In *Proceedings of the First World Congress on Mummy Studies,* 505–12. Tenerife, Canary Islands: Museo Arqueologico y Etnologico, 1995.

Proefke, Mark, and Kenneth Rinehart. "Analysis of an Egyptian Mummy Resin by

Mass Spectrometry." *Journal of the American Mass Spectrometry Society* 3 (1992): 582–89.

Proefke, Mark L., Kenneth L. Rinehart, Mastura Raheel, Stanley H. Ambrose, and Sarah U. Wisseman. "Probing the Mysteries of Ancient Egypt: Chemical Analysis of a Roman Period Egyptian Mummy." *Analytical Chemistry* 64, no. 2 (1992): 105A–111A.

Wisseman, Sarah U. "Imaging the Past: Nondestructive Analysis of an Egyptian Mummy." In *Ancient Technologies and Archaeological Materials,* ed. Sarah U. Wisseman and Wendell S. Williams, 217–34. Langhorne, Pa.: Gordon and Breach Science Publishers, 1994. Nontechnical summary of the project, written for undergraduates.

Wisseman, Sarah, Linda Klepinger, Richard Keen, Mastura Raheel, and Joseph Barkmeier. "Interdisciplinary Analysis of a Roman Period Egyptian Mummy." In *Archaeometry '90,* ed. E. Pernicka and G. Wagner, 345–53. Basel: Birkhauser, 1990.

Wright, Karen. "Tales from the Crypt." *Discover* 12, no. 7 (1991): 54–58.

THREE-DIMENSIONAL FACIAL RECONSTRUCTION

Evenhouse, Raymond, and Tony Stefanic. "Image Processing and Solid Modeling Recapture a Mummy's Face." *Advanced Imaging* (October 1992): 40–43.

Farkas, Leslie G. *Anthropology of the Head and Face in Medicine.* Oxford: Elsevier, 1981.

George, R. M. "The Lateral Craniographic Method of Facial Reconstruction." *Journal of Forensic Science* 32 (1987): 1305–30.

EMBALMING MATERIALS

Buckley, Stephen A., and Richard P. Evershed. "Organic Chemistry of Embalming Agents in Pharaonic and Graeco-Roman Mummies." *Nature* 413, no. 6858 (2001): 837–41.

Joseph, M. L. *Introduction to Textile Science.* 5th ed. New York: Holt Rinehart and Winston, 1986.

Lucas, Alfred. *Ancient Egyptian Materials and Industries.* 4th ed. Revised and enlarged by John R. Harris. London: Histories and Mysteries of Man, 1989.

Wisseman, Sarah. "Preserved for the Afterlife." *Nature* 413, no. 6858 (2001): 783–84.

EXPERIMENTAL MUMMIFICATION

Brier, Bob. *Egyptian Mummies: Unraveling the Secrets of an Ancient Art.* New York: William Morrow, 1994.

———. "A Thoroughly Modern Mummy." *Archaeology* (January/February 2001): 44–50.

WEB RESOURCES

Disease in ancient Egypt. ‹http://www.mja.com.au/public/issues/xmas98/ magee/magee.html› (on-line version of article in the *Medical Journal of Australia* by R. Magee)

"Egyptian Mummification" (Web page of the Spurlock Museum, University of Illinois at Urbana-Champaign). ‹http://www.spurlock.uiuc.edu/mummification/ index.html›

"How Stuff Works: Mummies." On-line article, 2001. ‹http://www.howstuffworks.com/ mummy.htm›

Mummy research at the Manchester Museum in Manchester, England. ‹http:// www.museum.man.ac.uk/collections/egyptology/egyptology_research.html›

The Research Archives of the Oriental Institute, University of Chicago. ‹http:// oilib.uchicago.edu/oilibcat.html›. Enter keywords "Egyptian Mummies."

Smithsonian Institution page on Egyptian mummification. ‹http://www.si.edu/ resource/faq/nmnh/mummies.htm›

A spin-off of the University of Illinois mummy project, put together by teachers in Champaign and Urbana, Illinois. ‹http://www.cmi.k12.il.us/Urbana/projects/ cybermummy/›

INDEX

tion; organs, internal; wrappings, mummy
endoscopy, 12
epiphyses, 11, 28, 51
Evenhouse, Raymond, 4, 37
evisceration, 6–7, 8, 14, 37. *See also* organs, internal

falcon, 9
Fayum, 15, 16, 19, 24, 51
flax, 45–47. *See also* linen
fractures, 10, 12, 14; of the jaw, 31; of the ribs, 28, 31, 50; of the skull, 14, 31, 34, 50, 51
funerary customs, 16, 17

Greeks, 16, 17, 24, 51
growth plates. *See* epiphyses

Harris, James, 11
Harris lines, 14, 30, 51; defined, 30
Hawara, 19, 21, 24
heart, 7, 13, 28, 31
Herodotus, 6–7, 8, 14, 42, 51, 52
Hibeh, el-, 19, 24, 26
Horus, 9, 22
human remains, treatment of, 1–3, 9

Iceman, Austrian, 1, 53
insects, 12, 39, 43, 45, 48, 51. *See also* beetles
Isis, 9

J. Paul Getty Museum, 24, 26
juniper oil, 8

ka, 5

Lady Teshat, 31
linen, 7, 8, 17, 24, 45–48, 51
lungs, 6, 12, 28, 31

Maat, 22
malaria, 13
malnutrition, 14, 51, 52
Manchester Museum, 11, 12, 24, 42, 45, 50, 52
Manchester University, 39. *See also* Manchester Museum

Merneptah, 36
mummies: fake, 13; Greek, 16; Peruvian, 1, 11
mummies, in museum collections: Boston, 12, 13, 18, 35, 40; Bristol, 13; Cairo, 11; Cambridge (England), 22; Chicago, 11; Cleveland, 13; Copenhagen, 24; Dayton, 13; Detroit, 11; Evanston, 24; Indianapolis, 13, 34, 35, 37; Kalamazoo, 37; Liverpool, 11; London, 13, 24, 52; Lyons, 8, 12; Malibu, 24; Manchester, 11, 12, 24, 39, 50, 52; Milwaukee, 13; Minneapolis, 31; Philadelphia, 12, 22, 50; Toronto, 13. *See also* Boston Museum of Fine Arts; British Museum, London; J. Paul Getty Museum; Manchester Museum; Spurlock Museum
mummification, 7–10, 13–14, 39, 50, 52, 53; economics of, 7, 8, 14, 17, 21–22. *See also* embalming; evisceration; organs, internal; wrappings, mummy
mummy: as a cure, 1; derivation of the term, 42; unwrappings of, 2, 3; use of in papermaking, 1; use of as locomotive fuel, 2
Murray, Margaret, 11

National Center for Supercomputing Applications (NCSA), 4, 35
Native American Graves Protection and Repatriation Act (NAGPRA), 3
natron, 7, 8, 52, 53
Nephthys, 9
Nut, 9, 22

organ packages, 8, 12, 27
organs, internal, 6–7, 8, 30, 50; intestines, 6; liver 6; stomach, 6. *See also* brain; heart; lungs; viscera
Osiris, 9, 22

packing materials, 6–7, 34, 51
parasites, intestinal, 12, 14. *See also* disease
Pennsylvania University Museum (PUM), 12, 22, 45, 51

Petrie, Sir Flinders, 10, 19, 21
pine pitch, 42
Plutarch, 8
polio, 11
portraits, mummy, 2, 9, 17, 19, 21, 22,
    41; on the Spurlock mummy, 22–24
preservation: of the body, 2, 5, 9; of
    mummies, 13, 14, 19, 52, 53; of por-
    traits, 22
prognathism, 36, 38, 51
provenance, 15, 19; of the Spurlock
    mummy, 15, 24
Ptolemaic period, 12, 17, 34
PUM II, 12
PUM IV, 39, 45, 51, 52

radiocarbon dating, 12, 40, 41, 43
radiography. See X-ray radiography
Ramesses II, 11
ramie, 45–48, 51
rebirth, 22
resins, 2, 7, 8, 9, 12, 13, 17, 19, 35, 40,
    48, 50, 51; analysis of, 12, 42–44.
    See also embalming, fluids
Roman period, 2, 9, 14, 17, 19, 22, 27,
    37, 39, 48, 51, 52; defined, 55
Romans, 15, 17, 24, 51
Rubayat, el-, 19

scanning electron microscopy (SEM),
    12, 45
schistosomiasis, 13
scoliosis, 14
Seqenenre Tao, 13
seriation, 10
Seth, 22
sex, of mummies, 4, 13, 34; of the
    Spurlock mummy, 4, 27, 48, 50
shabti, 5
silicosis, 12
Siptah, 11
Spurlock Museum, 11, 12, 21
stable isotope analysis, 48
stereolithography, 4, 38

stratigraphy, 10
stucco, 22, 24, 35; analysis of, 48–49,
    50

teeth, 12, 27, 36, 51; wear of, 11
textiles, analysis of, 11, 45–48. See
    also flax; linen; ramie
three-dimensional reconstruction, 3,
    11, 12, 30, 31, 35–38; sculptural, 4,
    37–38, 51; volumetric rendering, 4,
    35–37, 51
Thutmosis IV, 10
tomb robbers, 1
trichinosis, 13
Two Brothers, 11–12

ultrasound, 4, 38
ultraviolet light, 22–23
University of Alexandria, 11
University of Illinois, 3, 9, 10, 11, 12
University of Maryland, 52
University of Michigan, 11
University of Minnesota, 50
University of Pennsylvania, 12, 39, 51
unwrapping, of mummies, 2, 3
ushabti. See shabti

viscera, 7, 8, 9, 14, 42, 52. See also
    organs, internal

wadjet, eyes, 22
waxes, 42
Wenuhotep, 13
wood. See board
wrappings, mummy, 3,4, 6–9, 12, 13,
    14, 19, 21, 28, 30, 31, 35, 39, 42, 50;
    analysis of, 45–48. See also em-
    balming; mummification; textiles,
    analysis of

X-ray radiography, 10, 11, 27–30, 34,
    40, 50; defined, 10. See also X rays
X rays, 10, 11, 13, 27, 28, 51, 53

SARAH U. WISSEMAN is the director of the Program on Ancient Technologies and Archaeological Materials (ATAM) at the University of Illinois at Urbana-Champaign. She is the author of numerous articles and essays appearing in professional journals and exhibition catalogs.

**Indianapolis
Marion County
Public Library**

Renew by Phone
269-5222

Renew on the Web
www.imcpl.org

For general Library information
please call 269-1700.

#64124 Highsmith® Inc. 2003

'0 3